The Ultimate Dog Food Cookbook

Recipes for Easy to Make, Healthy Dog Food

Table of Contents

Introduction 4

    Turkey Veggie 6

    Beef Veggie 9

    Salmon Veggie 12

    Meaty Mix 14

    Slow Cooker Chicken 17

    Fall Specialty 19

    Orange Indulgence 21

    The Turkey Basics 23

    The Chicken Basics 25

    Doggy Burgers 27

    Turkey Burgers 29

    Beef Stew 31

    Chicken Stew 33

    Slow Cooker Veggie 35

    Vegan Dog Food 37

    Creamy Chicken and Vegetable 39

    Creamy Fruit and Vegetable 41

    Summer Smoothie 43

    Berry Smoothie 45

    Dog Pops 47

    Frozen Peanut Butter Cubes 49

Pumpkin Treats 51

Dog Crunchies 53

Turkey Jerky 55

Fruit and Veggie Strips 57

Veggie Treats 59

Beef and Veggie Treats 61

Chicken Veggie Treats 63

Chicken Chili 65

Pup Chili 67

Introduction

When you read the label on your dog's food, you may be surprised to find ingredients that you may not even be able to pronounce. Ingredients that are listed just as "meat" are also questionable as you really have no way of knowing what that meat is. The easy solution to feeding your dog healthy delicious food- make it yourself! It really isn't hard and you will rest assured knowing that your pup is getting the nutritious diet that they deserve.

I wanted to write this dog food cookbook after thinking a lot about what I was feeding my dog. I cook every night for my family and isn't our dog part of the family? He deserved homemade food too! As someone who has little extra time, this seemed like a challenge at first but then I found out how simple it is to make dog food that my pup would love. Most recipes take under 15 minutes (some even as quick as 5 minutes!) making them faster than most normal recipes.

The ingredients in each dog food recipe has been carefully checked to make sure that they are healthy for dogs and each recipe has been taste tested but multiple pups- they all approve! So what type of food will you make for your dog first? Some basic chicken dinner? Maybe a summer smoothie? Or possibly start off with a dog burger- they will all be winners! Call your dog over and let them know that soon, they will be eating homemade, delicious food every day!

Turkey Veggie

If your pup is a big fan of turkey but also love to chow down on veggies, then this is the recipe for you! Make a big batch of this recipe and portion it into freezer safe bags to use later.

Yield: 8 cups of food

Active Time: 30 minutes

Ingredients:

- 1 1/2 pounds ground Turkey
- 2 cups spinach
- 1 cup grated zucchini
- 3/4 cup diced or shredded carrots (frozen of fresh)
- 1 cup brown rice
- 1 Tbsp olive oil

Directions:

1. Begin by cooking the brown rice according to the package directions Once cooked, set the rice aside to cook and proceed with the recipe.

2. Using a large pot, heat the oil until it begins to shimmer. Once hot, add the turkey to the pot and break up the pieces using a rubber spatula or wooden spoon.

3. Cook the turkey, stirring frequently for about 5 minutes or until there is not pink left and the turkey is nicely browned.

4. Add the remaining ingredients and stir until cooked. The spinach should be wilted and the carrots and zucchini soft.

5. Turn the heat off of the stove and add the cooked rice to the turkey mixture. Stir everything together and allow to cool.

Beef Veggie

Lean ground beef is very good for your meat eating pup but always opt for a nice lean version. Full of veggies, brown rice and healthy meat, this is a food that you will feel good about giving to your dog.

Yield: 8 cups of food

Active Time: 30 minutes

Ingredients:

- 1 1/2 pounds lean ground beef
- 2 cups spinach
- 1 cup grated zucchini
- 3/4 cup diced or shredded carrots (frozen of fresh)
- 1 cup brown rice
- 1/2 cup frozen peas
- 1 Tbsp olive oil

Directions:

1. Begin by cooking the brown rice according to the package directions Once cooked, set the rice aside to cook and proceed with the recipe.

2. Using a large pot, heat the oil until it begins to shimmer. Once hot, add the ground beef to the pot and break up the pieces using a rubber spatula or wooden spoon.

3. Cook the lean ground beef, stirring frequently for about 5 minutes or until there is not pink left and the turkey is nicely browned.

4. Add the remaining ingredients and stir until cooked. The spinach should be wilted and the carrots and zucchini soft.

5. Turn the heat off of the stove and add the cooked rice to the turkey mixture. Stir everything together and allow to cool.

Salmon Veggie

Dogs love salmon. It may seem surprising but once you put a bowl of this food down in front of your pup, you will see how much dogs love to eat this healthy fish!

Yield: 8 cups of food

Active Time: 30 minutes

Ingredients:

- 1 1/2 pounds salmon
- 2 cups spinach
- 1 cup grated zucchini
- 3/4 cup diced or shredded carrots (frozen of fresh)

- 1 cup brown rice
- 1 cup frozen corn kernels
- 1/2 cup frozen peas
- 1 Tbsp olive oil

Directions:

1. Begin by cooking the brown rice according to the package directions Once cooked, set the rice aside to cook and proceed with the recipe.

2. Using a large pot, heat the oil until it begins to shimmer. Once hot, add the salmon to the pot and cook for about 5 minutes on one side, flip the filets and cook for another 3 minutes on the other side.

3. Once the salmon is cooked, break it apart into flaky pieces using a fork or spatula.

4. Add the remaining ingredients and stir until cooked. The spinach should be wilted and the corn, peas and carrots soft.

5. Turn the heat off of the stove and add the cooked rice to the turkey mixture. Stir everything together and allow to cool.

Meaty Mix

Three Kings of meat makes this tasty meal super pup friendly. Your dog is going to beg for this food as it is full of flavor and healthy home cooked meat that your pup will love!

Yield: 8 cups of food

Active Time: 30 minutes

Ingredients:

- 1/2 pound ground Turkey
- 1/2 pound lean ground beef
- 1/2 pound lean ground chicken
- 2 cups spinach
- 1 cup grated zucchini
- 3/4 cup diced or shredded carrots (frozen of fresh)
- 1 cup brown rice
- 1 Tbsp olive oil

Directions:

1. Begin by cooking the brown rice according to the package directions Once cooked, set the rice aside to cook and proceed with the recipe.

2. Using a large pot, heat the oil until it begins to shimmer. Once hot, add the turkey, beef and chicken to the pot and break up the pieces using a rubber spatula or wooden spoon.

3. Cook the meats, stirring frequently for about 5 minutes or until there is not pink left and the turkey is nicely browned.

4. Add the remaining ingredients and stir until cooked. The spinach should be wilted and the carrots and zucchini soft.

5. Turn the heat off of the stove and add the cooked rice to the turkey mixture. Stir everything together and allow to cool.

Slow Cooker Chicken

While many people love the convenience of buying pre-made dog food, you can easily make your pups food in a slow cooker with very little effort. Throw all the ingredients in the crock pot and let it cook! Your pup will thank you when that pot is finally done!

Yield: About 16 cups

Active Time: 5 minutes

Ingredients

- 6 cups ground chicken (three pounds)
- 2 cups canned red kidney beans, liquid drained, beans rinsed
- 1 cup frozen chopped carrots
- 1 cup frozen peas
- 1 cup frozen, chopped sweet potato
- 1 cup green beans
- 2 cups brown rice
- 4 cups chicken broth

Directions:

1. Place all of the **Ingredients** into a slow cooker and stir slightly.

2. Cook on high for four hours, stirring occasionally if you are able. You can also opt to set the slow cooker to low heat and cook for 6 hours.

3. Let the food cool and serve or freeze for later!

Fall Specialty

Many people try to eat seasonal foods meaning anything that is readily available at that time of the year is what they choose to consume. Why not have your dog eat seasonally as well? This fall medley is perfect for that time of year when the leaves are changing color and the weather begins to cool.

Yield: About 16 cups

Active Time: 5 minutes

Ingredients

- 6 cups ground turkey (three pounds)
- 2 cups canned red kidney beans, liquid drained, beans rinsed
- 1 cup frozen chopped pumpkin
- 2 cups frozen brussel sprouts
- 1 cup frozen corn kernels
- 2 cups brown rice
- 4 cups chicken broth

Directions:

1. Place all of the **Ingredients** into a slow cooker and stir slightly.

2. Cook on high for four hours, stirring occasionally if you are able. You can also opt to set the slow cooker to low heat and cook for 6 hours.

3. Let the food cool and serve or freeze for later!

Orange Indulgence

Orange foods are full of antioxidants, vitamin C and generally extremely nutritious. This orange laden dog food will be one that your pup adores and, it is so easy to make, that you will love it too!

Yield: About 16 cups

Active Time: 5 minutes

Ingredients

- 6 cups ground chicken (three pounds)
- 2 cups canned garbanzo beans, liquid drained, beans rinsed
- 1 cup frozen chopped pumpkin
- 2 cups frozen carrots
- 1 cup peeled and chopped sweet potato
- 2 cups brown rice
- 4 cups water

Directions:

1. Place all of the **Ingredients** into a slow cooker and stir slightly.

2. Cook on high for four hours, stirring occasionally if you are able. You can also opt to set the slow cooker to low heat and cook for 6 hours.

3. Let the food cool and serve or freeze for later!

The Turkey Basics

If your dog has a sensitive stomach, is just recovering from being sick or simply likes a more basic food, opt for this classic. Not only is it easy to make but it is perfect for just about every dog- they will love it!

Yield: 8 cups of food

Active Time: 5 minutes

Ingredients

- 5 1/2 cups chicken broth (or water if your dog is sensitive to chicken)
- 1 1/2 pounds lean ground turkey

- 1/2 cup frozen carrots
- 1/2 cup frozen peas
- 2 1/2 cups brown rice

Directions:

1. Place all the **Ingredients** into a large pot and stir briefly.

2. Bring the mix to a boil over the high heat and then lower the heat to medium low and let the mix simmer for about 25 minutes.

3. Remove the pot from the heat and stir. The rice should be fully cooked and all the broth or water should be dissolved.

4. Allow the food to cool and then refrigerate or cool until your dog is ready to eat!

The Chicken Basics

Chicken is an inexpensive and delicious food to feed your dog. This simple recipe is so quick to make and your dog will gobble it right up!

Yield: 8 cups of food

Active Time: 5 minutes

Ingredients

- 5 1/2 cups chicken broth (or water if your dog is sensitive to chicken)
- 1 1/2 pounds lean ground chicken
- 1/2 cup frozen carrots
- 1/2 cup frozen peas
- 2 1/2 cups brown rice

Directions:

1. Place all the **Ingredients** in a large pot and stir briefly.

2. Bring the mix to a boil over the high heat and lower the heat to medium low and let the mix simmer for about 25 minutes.

3. Remove the pot from the heat and stir. The rice should be fully cooked and all the broth or water should be dissolved.

4. Allow the food to cool and then refrigerate or cool until your dog is ready to eat!

Doggy Burgers

If you love burgers, why not make them for your dog?! Your pup is just as likely to love a good burger as you so make a double batch of this recipe and freeze some for your pup later.

Yield: 6 Burgers

Active Time: 10 minutes

Ingredients

- 1 pound ground beef (opt for a leaner beef if possible)
- 2 eggs

- 1 cup oats
- 1 cup peas
- 1/2 cup carrots
- 1/4 cup parmesan cheese, grated
- 1/4 cup low fat cottage cheese

Directions:

1. Mix all the **Ingredients** together in a bowl. Use your hands to really ensure that everything is well mixed.

2. Form the burgers into patties and bake in a 350 degree oven for 10 minutes, flip them and then bake for another 5 minutes. Baking the burgers makes sure you use less oil however, grilling the burgers is also a great option.

3. Let the burger cool and give it to your pup! These also freeze well for use at a later date

Turkey Burgers

Turkey burgers are a healthy and nutritious way to feed your pup the same thing that you eat. Make sure to make these for your dog at your next barbecue to include them in the festivities!

Yield: 6 Burgers

Active Time: 10 minutes

Ingredients

- 1 pound ground turkey (opt for a leaner turkey if possible)
- 2 eggs
- 1 cup oats
- 1 cup peas
- 1/2 cup carrots
- 1/4 cup parmesan cheese, grated
- 1/4 cup low fat cottage cheese

Directions:

1. Mix all the **Ingredients** together in a bowl. Use your hands to really ensure that everything is well mixed.

2. Form the burgers into patties and bake in a 350 degree oven for 10 minutes, flip them over and bake for another 5 minutes. Baking the burgers makes sure you use less oil however, grilling the burgers is also a great option.

3. Let the burger cool and give it to your pup! These also freeze well for use at a later date

Beef Stew

There is nothing like a nice bowl of hearty stew on a cold night. Your dog will agree after one taste of this delicious beef stew made just for pups! Quick to make and easy to store, this stew is a winner.

Yield: 6 cups of stew

Active Time: 10 minutes

Ingredients:

- 1 pound ground beef
- 1 cup diced sweet potato

- 1/2 cup chopped carrots
- 1/2 cup chopped green beans
- 2 cups beef broth
- 4 cups water

Directions:

1. Add all of the **Ingredients** to a large saucepot and bring to a simmer over medium heat.

2. Simmer the stew for 30 minutes, stirring occasionally, until the potatoes are soft and the meat is no longer pink.

3. Cool the stew until it is room temperature and give a nice big bowl to your pup!

Chicken Stew

Tasty lean chicken makes this stew super healthy and perfect for your pup. You may even want to have a bowl to yourself as well!

Yield: 6 cups of stew

Active Time: 10 minutes

Ingredients:

- 1 pound ground chicken
- 1 cup diced sweet potato
- 1/2 cup Idaho potatoes, diced
- 1/2 cup chopped carrots
- 1/2 cup chopped green beans
- 4 cups water
- 2 cups beef broth

Directions:

1. Add all of the **Ingredients** to a large saucepot and bring to a simmer over medium heat.

2. Simmer the stew for 30 minutes, stirring occasionally, until the potatoes are soft and the meat is no longer pink.

3. Cool the stew until it is room temperature and give a nice big bowl to your pup!

Slow Cooker Veggie

If you are trying to incorporate more veggies into your dogs diet, this is the easiest (and tastiest) way to do so. It is also perfect for dogs who don't need to eat a lot of meat!

Yield: About 16 cups

Active Time: 5 minutes

Ingredients

- 2 cups canned red kidney beans, liquid drained, beans rinsed

- 2 cups frozen chopped carrots
- 1 cup diced sweet potato
- 1 cup diced Idaho potato
- 1 cup frozen peas
- 1 cup frozen, chopped sweet potato
- 1 cup green beans
- 2 cups brown rice
- 4 cups water

Directions:

1. Place all of the **Ingredients** into a slow cooker and stir slightly.

2. Cook on high for four hours, stirring occasionally if you are able. You can also opt to set the slow cooker to low heat and cook for 6 hours.

3. Let the food cool and serve or freeze for later!

Vegan Dog Food

If you don't want to feed your pup meat or your dog just doesn't like eating meat, give this vegan recipe a try. It is easy enough to make and will still give your dog a well balanced diet.

Yield: 7 Cups

Active Time: 10 minutes

Ingredients:

- 3 cups brown rice, cooked
- 3 cups millet, already cooked per package directions
- 1 cup chopped carrots
- 1 cup peas
- 1 cup chopped green beans
- 1/2 cup water

Directions:

1. In a large pot or Dutch oven, add the cooked rice and cooked millet along with the water. Stir to combine. Heat over medium heat until simmering and let cook for 5 minutes.

2. In a blender, mix the remaining **Ingredients** and blend until smooth. Add the pureed veggies to the grain mix and stir.

3. Serve to your pup while warm but not hot. Store in the fridge or freeze until ready to serve!

Creamy Chicken and Vegetable

This dish is comprised mostly of pureed veggies which means that is it nice and creamy- easy for a pup to eat! This is perfect for older dogs or any dog who has issues chewing

Yield: 7 cups of food

Active Time: 10 minutes

Ingredients:

- 3 cups brown rice, cooked
- 1 cup cooked ground chicken

- 3 cups millet, already cooked per package directions
- 1 cup chopped carrots
- 1 cup peas
- 1 cup chopped green beans
- 1/2 cup water

Directions:

1. In a large pot or Dutch oven, add the cooked rice and cooked millet along with the water. Stir to combine. Heat over medium heat until simmering and let cook for 5 minutes.

2. In a blender, mix the remaining **Ingredients** and blend until smooth. Add the pureed veggies to the grain mix and stir.

3. Serve to your pup while warm but not hot. Store in the fridge or freeze until ready to serve!

Creamy Fruit and Vegetable

This meal is almost like a smoothie for pups as it is full of tasty veggies and fruits as well. Your dog with go bananas for the bananas which give this dish a sweet flavor.

Yield: 7 cups of food

Active Time: 10 minutes

Ingredients:

- 3 cups brown rice, cooked
- 3 cups millet, already cooked per package directions
- 1 cup chopped carrots
- 2 bananas

- 1 cup peas
- 1 cup chopped green beans
- 1/2 cup water

Directions:

1. In a large pot or Dutch oven, add the cooked rice and cooked millet along with the water. Stir to combine. Heat over medium heat until simmering and let cook for 5 minutes.

2. In a blender, mix the remaining **Ingredients** and blend until smooth. Add the pureed veggies to the grain mix and stir.

3. Serve to your pup while warm but not hot. Store in the fridge or freeze until ready to serve!

Summer Smoothie

This is definitely a special treat for your dog that wouldn't necessarily qualify as a full meal. Think of it more as a snack or dessert for your pup. You could also give it a try too!

Yield: 8 cups

Active Time: 5 minutes

Ingredients:

- 1 cup chopped strawberries
- 1 cup cantaloupe
- 1 cup blueberries
- 2 whole bananas
- 2 cups cooked brown rice
- 1 cup water

Directions:

1. Place all **Ingredients** into a blender and puree until smooth. Add a little extra water if needed to make the mix thinner. If you would like the mix to be a little thicker for your pup, add a little more brown rice.

2. Serve to your dog cold, almost frozen to help them cool down in the summer heat.

3. Store in the fridge or freezer until ready to eat!

Berry Smoothie

Did you know that dogs love berries and they are a super healthy, nutritious snack for your pup? That's right! This smoothie is a fantastic snack for your dog and will be one they beg for.

Yield: 8 cups

Active Time: 5 minutes

Ingredients:

- 1 cup chopped strawberries
- 1 cup raspberries

- 1 cup blueberries
- 2 whole bananas
- 2 cups cooked brown rice
- 1 cup water

Directions:

1. Place all **Ingredients** into a blender and puree until smooth. Add a little extra water if needed to make the mix thinner. If you would like the mix to be a little thicker for your pup, add a little more brown rice.

2. Serve to your dog cold, almost frozen to help them cool down in the summer heat.

3. Store in the fridge or freezer until ready to eat!

Dog Pops

When the weather gets hot, dogs need an easy way to cool down. Why not treat your dog to a homemade popsicle?! They will love the taste of these pops and it will help them stay cool in hot weather.

Yield: 8 cups

Active Time: 5 minutes

Ingredients:

- 1 cup chopped strawberries
- 1 cup blueberries
- 1 whole banana, peeled and chopped
- 2 cups plain, whole milk yogurt

Directions:

1. Place all **Ingredients** into a blender and puree until smooth.

2. pour the mix into popsicle molds and freeze for about 5 hours or until hard.

3. Serve to your dog cold to help them cool down in the summer heat. Be sure to keep an eye on your dog as they lick the pop, don't let them swallow the whole thing!

4. Store in the freezer until ready to eat!

Frozen Peanut Butter Cubes

These super easy frozen treats are perfect to toss to your pup anytime they need a special treat. Nice and cold, these are great for a hot day when your dog could use something cool.

Yield: 36 cubes

Active Time: 5 minutes

Ingredients

- 1 cup peanut butter
- 1/4 cup water

- 1/4 cup whole milk plain yogurt

Directions:

1. Blend all the **Ingredients** together in a blender or food processor until smooth.

2. Pour into an ice cube tray or small silicone mold and freeze for 4 hours or until frozen solid.

3. Pop out a cube anytime you need a treat for your dog!

Pumpkin Treats

A fall favorite that your dog will absolutely love. These pumpkin frozen treats are a breeze to put together and your dog will be ever thankful for such a tasty treat.

Yield: 36 cubes

Active Time: 5 minutes

Ingredients

- 1 cup chopped, cooked pumpkin
- 1/4 cup water
- 1/4 cup whole milk plain yogurt
- 1/8 tsp cinnamon

Directions:

1. Blend all the **Ingredients** together in a blender or food processor until smooth.

2. Pour into an ice cube tray or small silicone mold and freeze for 4 hours or until frozen solid.

3. Pop out a cube anytime you need a treat for your dog!

Dog Crunchies

If you need to make a snack that will be perfect for your pup, dehydrated fruit is the way to go. This will satisfy your pups need for crunch while still being super healthy.

Yield: 20 Snacks

Active Time: 10 minutes

Ingredients

- 20 Strawberries, thinly sliced
- 5 bananas, thinly sliced

Directions:

1. Thinly slice the strawberries and bananas and lay them on the trays of a dehydrator. Each piece of fruit should be separate and not overlapping or touching.

2. Dehydrate the fruit according to your manufacturer's directions. Store the treats in an airtight container and toss a few to your dog anytime they deserve a treat!

Turkey Jerky

If you like to give your dog a treat that will last a while, this is the one to give. This chewy, healthy meat will keep your pup busy for a while so toss them a jerky and know that they will be happily munching away for at least a few minutes!

Yield: about 16 strips

Active Time: 5 minutes

Ingredients:

- 4 Turkey Breasts

Directions:

1. Slice the turkey breast into thing, 1/16 inch strips and place on a baking sheet lined with a silicone mat.

2. Bake the strips in a 200 degree F oven for two hours, flipping after 1 1/2 hour and cooking the remaining 30 minutes.

3. Cool the jerky and store in an airtight container in the refrigerator for up to two weeks.

Fruit and Veggie Strips

These treats are perfect for your dog and ideal to have on hand all the time. They are cheaper than treats you will get in the pet store and not loaded with **Ingredients** that you can't even pronounce! Bake a big batch of these treats as they will last a long time!

Yield: 40 Treats

Active Time: 15 minutes

Ingredients

- 1 Sweet potato, cooked and peeled

- 1 large banana
- 2 cups flour (preferably whole wheat)
- 1 cup chopped, cooked carrots
- 1/2 cup applesauce
- 3/4 cup oats
- 1/4 cup warm water

Directions:

1. Place the banana and sweet potato in a food processor and puree until smooth.

2. Add the remaining **Ingredients** into the food processor and pulse until a dough begins to form.

3. Roll the dough on a lightly floured surface to about 1/8 of an inch thick. Then, use a knife or pizza cutter to cut the dough into long strips.

4. Place the strips on a lined cookie sheet and bake in a 350 degree F oven for 25 minutes.

5. Break the strips into small pieces for your dog and serve once cooled.

Veggie Treats

All dogs love a good treat and most dog owners love to be able to toss their pup a treat and be assured that it is healthy. When you make these veggie treats, you will know every time you give your dog a snack that you are feeding them something nutritious!

Yield: 40 Treats

Active Time: 15 minutes

Ingredients

- 1 Sweet potato, cooked and peeled

- 2 cups flour (preferably whole wheat)
- 1 cup chopped, cooked carrots
- 1/2 cup peas
- 1/2 cup green beans
- 1/2 cup applesauce
- 3/4 cup oats
- 1/4 cup warm water

Directions:

1. Place the carrots and sweet potato in a food processor and puree until smooth.

2. Add the remaining **Ingredients** into the food processor and pulse until a dough begins to form.

3. Roll the dough on a lightly floured surface to about 1/8 of an inch thick. Then, use a knife or pizza cutter to cut the dough into long strips.

4. Place the strips on a lined cookie sheet and bake in a 350 degree F oven for 25 minutes.

5. Break the strips into small pieces for your dog and serve once cooled.

Beef and Veggie Treats

If your dog loves meat and just can't get enough meaty treats, then this is the recipe for you! Full of meat and speckled with veggies, you can feel good every time you give your dog one of these nutritious treats.

Yield: 20 treats

Active Time: 15 minutes

Ingredients

- 1 1/2 cups pureed, cooked beef
- 1/2 cup whole wheat flour
- 1/2 cup rolled oats
- 2 cups dry milk powder
- 1/2 cup cooked peas
- 1 cup water

Directions:

1. Mix all of the **Ingredients** together in a large bowl, stirring until everything is fully combined.

2. Scoop the mix onto a parchment lined cookie sheet using and ice cream scoop to ensure each treat is the same size.

3. Bake in a 350 degree F oven for 15 minutes.

4. Allow the treats to fully cool before tossing one to your pup.

5. Store the treats in the fridge, wrapped for up to 5 days.

Chicken Veggie Treats

Chicken is a very healthy meat to serve to your dog and now, with this recipe, you can give it as a treat as well. Full of tasty vegetables and healthy chicken, your dog will love snacking on these treats just as much as you will love making them.

Yield: 20 treats

Active Time: 15 minutes

Ingredients

- 1 1/2 cups pureed, cooked chicken
- 1/2 cup whole wheat flour
- 1/2 cup rolled oats

- 2 cups dry milk powder
- 1/2 cup cooked peas
- 1/2 cup cooked corn kernels
- 1 cup water

Directions:

1. Mix all of the **Ingredients** together in a large bowl, stirring until everything is fully combined.

2. Scoop the mix onto a parchment lined cookie sheet using and ice cream scoop to ensure each treat is the same size.

3. Bake in a 350 degree F oven for 15 minutes.

4. Allow the treats to fully cool before tossing one to your pup.

5. Store the treats in the fridge, wrapped for up to 5 days.

Chicken Chili

You aren't the only one who would enjoy a nice big bowl of chili- your dog would too! Full of beans, meat and veggies, this meal is filling and very nutritious, perfect for your four legged friend!

Yield: 8 cups

Active Time: 15 minutes

Ingredients

- 3 pounds chicken breast
- 1 can red kidney beans, drained and rinsed

- 1 can black beans, drained and rinsed
- 1/3 cup tomato paste
- 2 cups water
- 2 cups chicken broth

Directions:

1. Trim any fat off of the chicken breast and then cut it into small, one inch pieces. Place the chicken in sauté pan and sear for about 2 minutes on each side, just until the outside is no longer pink.

2. Move the chicken to a large pot and Add all the remaining **Ingredients**.

3. Bring the mix to a boil and simmer for ten minutes.

4. Remove from the heat and allow the chili to cool. Serve to your pup right away or store in the fridge or freezer to use at a later time!

Pup Chili

Ground beef, ground turkey and lots of beans makes this chili a protein packed treat. The veggies are a nice addition to put this chili into the "well balanced meal" category.

Yield: 10 cups

Active Time: 15 minutes

Ingredients

- 1 pound ground turkey
- 1 pounds ground lean beef
- 1 can red kidney beans, drained and rinsed
- 1 cup carrots, chopped
- 1/2 cup corn kernels
- 1/3 cup tomato paste
- 1 can black beans, drained and rinsed
- 2 cups water
- 2 cups chicken broth

Directions:

1. Place the ground beef and ground turkey in a non stick skillet and sear for about 5 minutes, breaking it apart with a spatula as it cooks.

2. Move the chicken to a large pot and Add all the remaining **Ingredients**.

3. Bring the mix to a boil and simmer for ten minutes.

4. Remove from the heat and allow the chili to cool. Serve to your pup right away or store in the fridge or freezer to use at a later time!

Made in the USA
Columbia, SC
27 June 2019